Inspiration: Write Every Day

Daily Inspiration for Writers

Kathleen O'Mara

Inspiration: Write Every Day

ISBN: 978-1470002633

For more information about this book or the author, visit:

http://www.kathleenomara.com

~ Dedicated to old friends, new friends
& writers who write ~

If necessity is the mother of invention, then frustration is the father of this book. I looked for this book in book stores and online, to no avail. Finally, like the little red hen, I gave in and wrote it. With prompting from some of my biggest fans, it's complete and ready for you, dear Reader/Writer.

This book is dedicated to writers who refuse to give into writer's block. The contents are designed specifically to prompt you through those moments or days that things just don't seem to be moving along as expect.

Each page is divided into four sections:
1)   Inspirational quotes from famous to extremely famous authors, all who spoke about writing.
2)   Thoughts to ponder or not, hopefully you'll have some reaction, thoughts of your own.
3)   The Today section makes a statement in the affirmative: agree or not, the point is to move forward.
4)   Prompt writing in whatever way possible, silly, serious, sensational, the choice is yours.

There are two kinds of books in my library. The books I read and the books I absolutely love. My most loved books have changed my way of thinking or way of life in some way. These favorite books are completely annotated.

Annotation brings our studies home to us. By noting in the margin, thoughts, references and other points to remember, we learn and grow in ways that are difficult and astounding. We grow and notice our growth at the same time.

I hope this book, your book, is filled with your thoughts, answers, arguments, doodles, underlines, stars, checks and more as you grow and become an even better writer.

Yes, yes, please write in this book.

January 1

Every great and original writer, in proportion as he is great and original, must himself create the taste by which he is to be relished.

~ William Wordsworth

Thought:

Why write?

Today:

I will not allow excuses to keep me from writing.

Prompt:

List Writing Goals for the Week, Month, Year: 1, 2, 3, 4, 5.

January 2

I'm against homogenized society because I want the cream to rise to the top.
~ Robert Frost

Thought:

Who is the heroine/hero? Why?

Today:

I will practice my trade: writing.

Prompt:

Create the mood for adventure.

January 3

A perfectly healthy sentence is extremely rare. For the most part we miss the hue and fragrance of the thought; as if we could be satisfied with the dews of the morning or evening without their colors, or the heavens without their azure.
~ Henry David Thoreau

Thought:

Make Magic Meaningful

Today:

I recognize my talent.

Prompt:

Describe the character's favorite book.

January 4

The Writer writes in order to teach himself, to understand himself, to satisfy himself; the publishing of his ideas, though it brings gratification, is a curious anticlimax.

~ Alex Kazin

Thought:

Preparation to write becomes the crux of the matter. Write what?

Today:

The time to put energy into my writing is now.

Prompt:

Write one paragraph about the weather.

January 5

Reading is to the mind what exercise is to the body.
~ Sir Richard Steele

Thought:

Revise, Revise, Revise

Today:

I will take care of business.

Prompt:

Write a description of your least favorite teacher.

January 6

I would define, in brief, the poetry of words as the rhythmical creation of beauty.
                    ~ Edgar Allan Poe

Thought:

Does the paragraph bring the room into view?

Today:

I will edit to improve the piece.

Prompt:

Explain Why.

January 7

Hard writing makes easy reading.
                              ~ Wallace Stegner

Thought:

Is the obstacle compelling?

Today:

I will write a query.

Prompt:

How does it smell?

January 8

Books want to be born: I never make them. They come to me
and insist on being written, and on being such and such.
~ Samuel Butler

Thought:

Description becomes important for placement in time & space.

Today:

I will find a sentence I enjoy.

Prompt:

Write your grandfather's history.

January 9

When we see a natural style we are quite amazed and delighted, because we expected to see an author and find a man.

~ Blaise Pascal

Thought:

Magistrate, hallucinate, discarnate, liberate, accommodate, terminate, exaggerate, reverberate…

Today:

I will acknowledge my skills as a writer and share them.

Prompt:

Write a description of what you see in the mirror.

January 10

So many men so many questions.
                    ~ Publis Terentius Afer

Thought:

How would a second grader say it?

Today:

I will find a writer's group and attend a meeting.

Prompt:

Describe the ultimate gadget.

January 11

The function of genius is to furnish cretins with ideas twenty years later.

~ Louis Aragon

Thought:

The causal chain moves the story from A to B to C.

Today:

I will help another writer improve their writing.

Prompt:

Describe the ultimate NOTHING.

January 12

Seek ye good things of the mind, the rest will be supplied.
~ Sir Francis Bacon

Thought:

List words in groups by age or grade.

Today:

I will write something funny.

Prompt:

Write an obituary.

January 13

Life can't ever really defeat a writer who is in love with writing, for life itself is a writer's lover until death – fascinating, cruel, lavish, warm, cold, treacherous, constant.
~ Edna Ferber

Thought:

Make an appeal to the senses.

Today:

I will reach deep inside myself for the perfect world.

Prompt:

Write 5 things you learned in high school.

January 14

Experience is one thing you can't get for nothing.
~ Oscar Wilde

Thought:

Exclamation Points = You!

Today:

I will make a commitment to a piece of work.

Prompt:

Describe COLD.

January 15

I disapprove of what you say, but I defend to the death your right to say it.

~ Voltaire

Thought:

Understand the genre.

Today:

I will complete my daily goal.

Prompt:

List 3 things your father said.

January 16

If you want to get rich from writing, write the sort of thing that's read by persons who move their lips when they're reading to themselves.
~ Don Marquis

Thought:

Write a memorable ending: not necessarily happily ever after but an ending the reader affirms.

Today:

I accept I had to overcome rejection letters.

Prompt:

Write a 15 word poem.

January 17

A day's work is a day's work, neither more nor less, and the man who does it needs a day's sustenance a night's repose and due leisure, whether he be a painter or a ploughman.
~ George Bernard Shaw

Thought:

Cruelty makes problems.

Today:

I will share my opinion.

Prompt:

Describe the sound of silence.

January 18

Good books, like good friends, are few and chosen; the more select, the more enjoyable.
                    ~ Louisa May Alcott

Thought:

Fully written material leaves little room for misinterpretation.

Today:

I will fact check.

Prompt:

What does she say to her hair dresser?

January 19

Writing is utter solitude, the descent into the cold abyss
of oneself.

~ Franz Kafka

Thought:

Explore the complexities of the character by changing the
context of the scene.

Today:

I will make an effort to write well.

Prompt:

Write 3 qualities of a best friend.

January 20

Without knowing the force of words, it is impossible to know men.

~ Confucius

Thought:

Language expands and contracts with use.

Today:

I will remember to eat lunch.

Prompt:

Describe his clothes.

January 21

Loafing is the most productive part of a writer's life.
~ James Norman Hall

Thought:

How important is a comma?

Today:

I accept constructive criticism.

Prompt:

Describe a bee flying to a honey tree.

January 22

I am irritated by my own writing. I am like a violinist whose ear is true, but whose fingers refuse to reproduce precisely the sound he hears within.
~ Gustave Flaubert

Thought:

Not all writing is created equal. Find your niche.

Today:

I will get out of the way and let the muse speak through me.

Prompt:

Write 3 things you love about your protagonist.

January 23

Of writing well the source and fountainhead is wise thinking.
~ Horace

Thought:

Does the color make a difference to the story?

Today:

I accept my writing obsession.

Prompt:

Describe why she cried.

January 24

And by the way, everything in life is writable about if you have the outgoing guts to do it, and the imagination to improvise. The worst enemy to creativity is self-doubt.
~ Sylvia Plath

Thought:

Design the Scene, the Place, the Taste, the Smell, the Sound and the Sight.

Today:

I will work hard.

Prompt:

When the bell rings…

January 25

No author dislikes to be edited as much as he dislikes not to be published.
~ Russell Lynes

Thought:

Dialogue needs to advance the plot.

Today:

I will improve my skills.

Prompt:

Dialog between mother & son.

January 26

Never apologize for showing feeling. When you do so, you apologize for showing the truth.
~ Benjamin Disraeli

Thought:

What is the motivation for the characters to act?

Today:

I will not waste time.

Prompt:

Think pink... Write it...

January 27

Words make love with one another.
                    ~ Andre Breton

Thought:

Writers' groups help critique incomplete projects.

Today:

I will keep an open mind.

Prompt:

Write a paragraph about politics from the other side.

January 28

Our life is frittered away by detail. Simplify, simplify.
~ Henry David Thoreau

Thought:

Edit out the unnecessary.

Today:

I am ready to learn something new.

Prompt:

Write a first paragraph about a plane crash.

January 29

Oh for a book and a shady nook.
                    ~ John Wilson

Thought:

When you hit a wall, turn left.

Today:

I will surrender control to an editor.

Prompt:

Write a love note.

January 30

Don't ever get to feeling important about yourself…
an editor can only get as much out of an author as the author
has in him.
~ Maxwell Perkins

Thought:

Write words daily.

Today:

I will challenge myself to write clearly and concisely.

Prompt:

Describe a car.

January 31

Don't waste yourself in rejection, not bark against the bad, but chant the beauty of good.
~ Ralph Waldo Emerson

Thought:

Change thoughts and actions to reveal gender bias.

Today:

I will join another writer for coffee or tea.

Prompt:

Describe the least likely to succeed.

February 1

Easy is to occupy a place in a telephone book. Difficult is to occupy someone's heart; know that you're really loved.
~ Carlos Drummond de Andrade

Thought:

What is the ration of the pace of the sentence to the pace of the story?

Today:

I will focus on my project.

Prompt:

Write a limerick.

February 2

Experience means conflict, our natures being what they are
conflict means drama.
~ Allen Tate

Thought:

Character flaws work into the story.

Today:

I will let the piece set for a while.

Prompt:

Write a reason for music.

February 3

Love truth and pardon error.
                              ~ Voltaire

Thought:

Edit for spelling errors.

Today:

I will remove some clutter from my writing.

Prompt:

Describe an awful taste.

February 4

Everybody has to write out of rage sometimes.
                    ~ Amy Clampitt

Thought:

Writers read.

Today:

I will write what I know.

Prompt:

Write a letter to Death.

February 5

The world is full of willing people, some are willing to work,
the rest are willing to let them.
~ Robert Frost

Thought:

Adjectives may distract the reader from the plot.

Today:

I will start with one word.

Prompt:

Describe the hero/heroine.

February 6

Most editors are failed writer – but so are most writers.
~ T.S. Eliot

Thought:

Important details are important to the story.

Today:

I'm working on my best work ever!

Prompt:

Write 10 favorite words.

February 7

Many (novels) have a beginning, a muddle and an end.
~ Philip Larkin

Thought:

Think: Point of View.

Today:

I will remember the lessons I've learned.

Prompt:

Describe the Stars.

February 8

Becoming the reader is the essence of becoming a writer.
~ John O'Hara

Thought:

Outline the story.

Today:

I will improve my word choice.

Prompt:

Describe the world in black & white.

February 9

Fill your paper with the breathings of your heart.
~ William Wordsworth

Thought:

Learn from failure.

Today:

I am free to write what I want.

Prompt:

Explain why you are late.

February 10

I like to write when I feel spiteful;   it's like having a
good sneeze.
> ~ D. H. Lawrence

Thought:

Buy and Read a book written by a local author.

Today:

I am happy to write.

Prompt:

Describe dessert.

February 11

The difficult of literature is not to write, but to write what you mean.

~ Robert Louis Stevenson

Thought:

Character obsession gives reason to the absurd.

Today:

I love my writing life.

Prompt:

Describe pain.

February 12

The reason one writes isn't the fact he wants to say something.
He writes because he has something to say.
~ F. Scott Fitzgerald

Thought:

Edit for over used words.

Today:

I will ask for help.

Prompt:

List 3 things you hate about your best friend.

February 13

To be a well favored man is the gift of fortune, but to write or read comes by nature.

~ William Shakespeare

Thought:

Writers are observers who tell what they see.

Today:

I need not judge my work.

Prompt:

Think Blue… Write it…

February 14

The best way out is through.
~ Robert Frost

Thought:

Is the ending predictable?

Today:

I will research something new.

Prompt:

Write a paragraph about Love.

February 15

How much easier it is to be critical than to be correct.
~ Benjamin Disraeli

Thought:

What is the best moment in the writing process?

Today:

I trust I'm making progress.

Prompt:

Describe your characters eyes.

February 16

Literature is an occupation in which you have to keep proving
your talent to people who have none.
~ Jules Renard

Thought:

Assume Nothing.

Today:

I will pay attention to my needs.

Prompt:

Describe the phone.

February 17

No one knows what he can do till he tries.
                            ~ Publilis Syrus

Thought:

What binds the characters together in the scene or story?

Today:

I choose to write.

Prompt:

Explain the reason for a ticket.

February 18

I was not looking for my dreams to interpret my life, but rather for my life to interpret my dreams.
~ Susan Sontag

Thought:

Summarize the plot.

Today:

I will know the grammar rules before I break them.

Prompt:

List 3 needs and 3 wants. Explain the difference.

February 19

No man should ever publish a book until he has first read it to a woman.
> ~ Van Wyck Brooks

Thought:

Kids like to read about characters who are slightly older.

Today:

I will learn a new word.

Prompt:

Write two sentences without the verb "to be."

February 20

If my doctor told me I had only six minutes to live, I wouldn't brood. I'd type a little faster.
                    ~ Isaac Asimov

Thought:

Is the conflict age appropriate for the audience?

Today:

I will seek a new source.

Prompt:

If you were an animal what would that be and why.

February 21

A great book should leave you with many experiences, and slightly exhausted at the end. You live several lives while reading it.

~ William Styron

Thought:

Inspiration comes from life.

Today:

I will face my fear.

Prompt:

Write the motivation for your hero.

February 22

Words are the most powerful drug used by mankind.
~ Rudyard Kipling

Thought:

Retell a favorite story.

Today:

I will ask, "how important is it?"

Prompt:

Describe a fight.

February 23

He who has begun is half done. Dare to be wise; begin!
~ Horace

Thought:

Adjectives may contribute important information.

Today:

If I feel overwhelmed, I will look at smaller portions of the project.

Prompt:

Justify loving a bad character.

February 24

Preachers in pulpits talked about what a great message is the book. No matter what you do, somebody always inputs meaning into your books.
~ Theodor Seuss Geisel

Thought:

Create a challenge.

Today:

I feel comfortable as a writer.

Prompt:

List 5 reasons to write.

February 25

The first chapter sells the book; the last chapter sells the next book.

~ Mickey Spillane

Thought:

Polish the manuscript.

Today:

I will promote my work.

Prompt:

Describe a jungle.

February 26

He who spares the wicked injures the good.
~ Seneca

Thought:

What's a writing schedule?

Today:

I will face the challenge.

Prompt:

List 5 chores for a teenager.

February 27

There are three rules for writing the novel. Unfortunately, no one knows what they are.
~ William Somerset Maugham

Thought:

Craft a query letter to an agent.

Today:

I will take notes.

Prompt:

Explain life to a three year old.

February 28

A word is not the same with one writer as with another.
One tears it from his guts. The other pulls it out of his
overcoat pocket.

~ Charles Peguy

Thought:

Think visually.

Today:

I have the discipline to write today.

Prompt:

He said …

February 29

A great deal of talent is lost to the world for want of a little courage.

~ Sidney Smith

Thought:

Dialogue is not typical conversation.

Today:

I will learn from a mistake.

Prompt:

Describe the room you had as a child.

March 1

A writer needs loneliness, and he gets his share of it. He needs love, and he gets shared and unshared love. He needs friendship. In fact, he needs the universe. To be a writer is, in a sense, to be a day-dreamer – to be living a kind of double life.
~ Jorge Luis Borges

Thought:

Read Aloud.

Today:

I will read the newspaper.

Prompt:

Describe birth.

March 2

Say all you have to say in the fewest possible words, or your
reader will sure to skip them; and in the plainest possible
words or he will certainly misunderstand the message.
~ John Rushkin

Thought:

Prepare market information for the project.

Today:

I will outline my project.

Prompt:

Write 2 sentences about a scientist.

March 3

It is not fair to ask of others what you are unwilling to
do yourself.
~ Eleanor Roosevelt

Thought:

What else is at the book store?

Today:

I will not waste energy.

Prompt:

Describe a first kiss.

March 4

Man is what he reads.
> ~ Joseph Brodsky

Thought:

Understand the difference between passive & active language.

Today:

I remind myself to do better, choose better.

Prompt:

Spell 5 letter words vertically. Use each letter to start a description of that word.

March 5

The scholar who cherishes the love of comfort is not fit to be deemed a scholar.

~ Confucius

Thought:

Avoid Cliché!

Today:

I am willing to learn to write better.

Prompt:

Describe a bubble.

March 6

It is the little writer rather than the great writer who seems never to quote, and the reason is that he is never really doing anything else.
~ Havelock Ellis

Thought:

Choose an unusual or improbable theme.

Today:

I will stop struggling.

Prompt:

Write a review of the perfect book.

March 7

For me, a page of good prose is where one hears the rain [and] the noise of battle.

~ John Cheever

Thought:

Increase Intensity.

Today:

I will contribute to my writing group.

Prompt:

Describe the Queens' jewelry.

March 8

The good writing of any age has always been the product of someone's neurosis, and we'd have a mighty dull literature if all the writers that came along were a bunch of happy chuckleheads.

~ William Styron

Thought:

Notice the rhythm of the language.

Today:

I depend upon others.

Prompt:

Describe an injury.

March 9

No act of kindness, no matter how small is ever wasted.
~ Aesop

Thought:

Outline a plan.

Today:

I will use punctuation correctly.

Prompt:

Describe lunch for a tiger.

March 10

Better to write for yourself and have no public, than to write
for the public and have no self.

~ Cyril Connolly

Thought:

Make every word count.

Today:

I will delete useless versions.

Prompt:

Write 5 reasons to stay.

March 11

Your descendants shall gather your fruit.
~ Virgil

Thought:

Write a cover letter.

Today:

I acknowledge my mind's power.

Prompt:

Write a story about air.

March 12

Experience has shown, and a true philosophy will always show, that a vast, perhaps the larger portion of the truth arises from the seemingly irrelevant.
~ Edgar Allan Poe

Thought:

Read Classics.

Today:

I will not wait. I will write today.

Prompt:

Think Purple...Write it...

March 13

Reading usually precedes writing and the impulse to write is almost always is fired by reading. Reading, the love of reading, is what makes you dream of becoming a writer.
~ Susan Sontag

Thought:

Is the dialogue in character?

Today:

I will correct mistakes.

Prompt:

Use 3 commas in a sentence.

March 14

To begin, begin.

> ~ William Wordsworth

Thought:

Each set of characters have a subplot of their own.

Today:

I will find the right words.

Prompt:

Describe the taste of chocolate.

March 15

One man is as good as another until he has written a book.
~ Benjamin Jowett

Thought:

Composition is the intentional arrangement of words to express an idea.

Today:

I will encourage a young writer.

Prompt:

Write a letter of thanks.

March 16

Invention, it must be humbly admitted, does not consist in creating out of a void, but out of chaos; the materials must in the first place be afforded; it can give form to dark, shapeless substances, but cannot bring into being the substance itself.
~ Mary Shelley

Thought:

Characters don't get along with everyone.

Today:

Begin.

Prompt:

Write 5 words to describe water.

March 17

So often is the virgin sheet of paper more real than what one
has to say, and so often one regrets having married it.
~ Harold Acton

Thought:

Is there a moral to the story?

Today:

I will proof read.

Prompt:

Explain the reason for fences.

March 18

Self-pity is our worst enemy and if we yield to it, we can never do anything good in the world.
~ Helen Keller

Thought:

Keep a journal.

Today:

I will meet the deadline.

Prompt:

Write a paragraph about a baby.

March 19

Prune what is turgid, elevate what is commonplace, arrange what is disorderly, introduce rhythm where the language is harsh, modify where it is too absolute.
~ Marcus Fabius Quintilianus

Thought:

Character gestures need to be correct for place and time.

Today:

Writing is a habit.

Prompt:

Describe the sounds on a playground.

March 20

Almost anyone can be an author; the business is to collect money and fame from this state of being.

~ A.A. Milne

Thought:

Table of Contents

Today:

I am calm.

Prompt:

Quote a famous person.

March 21

Much speech is one thing, well-timed speech is another.
~ Sophocles

Thought:

Revenge is a good motivation.

Today:

I need only be willing.

Prompt:

Describe fast.

March 22

The writer who possesses the creative gift owns something of which he is not always master – something that at times strangely wills and works for itself.

~ Charlotte Bronte

Thought:

Who is telling the story?

Today:

I choose this life.

Prompt:

Write a journal entry.

March 23

Always do right. This will gratify some people and astonish the rest.
~ Mark Twain

Thought:

Conflict or Competition

Today:

I will not wallow in self-pity.

Prompt:

Write a dialog between a father & daughter.

March 24

It takes courage to grow up and become who really are.
~ e.e. cummings

Thought:

Epiphanies need to make sense.

Today:

I will get results.

Prompt:

Write 3 reasons you write.

March 25

A writer never has a vacation. For a writer, life consists of
either writing or thinking about writing.
~ Eugene Ionesco

Thought:

Call the publisher to verify the submission editor's name.

Today:

I will call a friend.

Prompt:

Describe a butterfly.

March 26

Abuse is often of service. There is nothing so dangerous to an author as silence.
~ Samuel Johnson

Thought:

Tell versus Show or Show versus Tell.

Today:

Write with wild abandon.

Prompt:

Describe an exciting moment.

March 27

A synonym is a word you use when you can't spell the other.
~ Baltazar Gracian

Thought:

Increase vocabulary by one word.

Today:

I will run out of time for distraction.

Prompt:

Write a first paragraph about a wedding.

March 28

An author in his book must be like God in the universe,
present everywhere and visible nowhere.
~ Gustave Flaubert

Thought:

Review the manuscript thoughtfully.

Today:

I will invite a friend to dinner.

Prompt:

Describe the smell of rain.

March 29

It's none of their business that you have to learn to write. Let them think you were born that way.
~ Ernest Hemingway

Thought:

Annotate.

Today:

I will have a strong vision of my project.

Prompt:

Write a poem about grease.

March 30

Never discourage anyone who continually makes progress, no matter how slow.

~ Plato

Thought:

Who is your audience?

Today:

I put criticism in perspective.

Prompt:

List 10 beautiful things.

March 31

As for my next book, I am going to hold myself from writing it till I have it impending in me: grown heavy in my mind like a ripe pear; pendant, gravid, asking to be cut or it will fall.
~ Virginia Woolf

Thought:

Write in a dialect to create believable characters.

Today:

Vocabulary is important.

Prompt:

Describe the scent of a pine tree.

April 1

If you would write emotionally, be first unemotional. If you
would move your readers to tears, do not let them see you cry.
~ James J. Kilpatrick

Thought:

Edit out meaningless words.

Today:

I will put good energy into my writing.

Prompt:

Write 5 feelings.

April 2

...it will not always happen that the success of poet is proportionate to his labor.

~ Samuel Johnson

Thought:

Narrow your search of possible to probable publishers.

Today:

I will change for the better.

Prompt:

Explain rain.

April 3

Every murderer is probably somebody's old friend.
~ Agatha Christie

Thought:

Play with Rhyming.

Today:

I will listen to my inner voice.

Prompt:

Describe a tree.

April 4

I cannot live without books.
                    ~ Thomas Jefferson

Thought:

Outline a mystery.

Today:

I will share my knowledge with others.

Prompt:

List 5 qualities of a good book.

April 5

The story I am writing exists, written in absolutely perfect fashion, some place, in the air. All I must do is find it, and copy it.

~ Jules Renard

Thought:

Set goals.

Today:

I will love my characters.

Prompt:

List 10 ways to walk.

April 6

To be a well-favored man is the gift of fortune; but to write and read comes by nature.
~ William Shakespeare

Thought:

Edit for pronouns.

Today:

I will buy a book by a new author.

Prompt:

Think yellow… write it…

April 7

I shall never be ashamed of citing a bad author if the line is good.

~ Seneca

Thought:

Interview a person.

Today:

I enjoy solitude.

Prompt:

Write a poem about May.

April 8

The secret of getting ahead is getting started.
~ Agatha Christie

Thought:

What is the attraction to writing?

Today:

I acknowledge myself for taking risks.

Prompt:

Describe walking in muddy water.

April 9

Yesterday is today's memory, tomorrow is today's dream.
~ Kahlil Gibran

Thought:

Double-check variant words.

Today:

I appreciate the people who help me.

Prompt:

Describe the sounds in a kitchen.

April 10

Some of my youthful readers are developing wonderful imaginations. This pleases me.
~ L. Frank Baum

Thought:

Attend a workshop.

Today:

I will acknowledge the good and the bad in my writing.

Prompt:

Describe what's in the refrigerator.

April 11

Writing is easy. All you do is sit staring at a blank sheet of paper until drops of blood form on your forehead.
~ Gene Fowler

Thought:

Use Character worksheets or drawings to keep the character consistent.

Today:

I will enjoy my freedom.

Prompt:

Describe a shocking event.

April 12

Pleasure in the job puts perfection in the work.
~ Aristotle

Thought:

Edit misdirection in dialogue.

Today:

I am not afraid to follow my dream.

Prompt:

Describe a table.

April 13

They can do all because they think they can.
~ Virgil

Thought:

Check character names throughout the story.

Today:

I will find time to relax.

Prompt:

Describe the Ocean.

April 14

The writer walks out of his room in a daze. He wants a drink.
He needs it.
~ Roald Dahl

Thought:

Double check homonyms or other misused words.

Today:

I will walk outside.

Prompt:

List 5 funny words/ things.

April 15

Don't tell me the moon is shining; show me the glint of light
on broken glass.
~ Anton Chekov

Thought:

Check tense: past, present, future

Today:

I will accept my writing as my best.

Prompt:

Describe the hat she wore.

April 16

The most beautiful things are those that madness prompts and reason writes.

~ Andre Gide

Thought:

Carry paper & pen everywhere.

Today:

I will improve one sentence at a time.

Prompt:

Describe the scent of a flower.

April 17

A critic can only review the book he has read, not the one
which the writer wrote.
~ Mignon McLaughlin

Thought:

Study the books you enjoy.

Today:

I choose to write well.

Prompt:

Describe a voice.

April 18

Finish each day and be done with it. You've done what
you could.
~ Ralph Waldo Emerson

Thought:

Outline a biography.

Today:

I will listen to a reading.

Prompt:

Explain why life is easy for him/her.

April 19

Writing, I think, is not apart from living. Writing is a kind of double living. The writer experiences everything twice. Once is reality and once in that mirror which waits always before or behind.

~ Catherine Bowen

Thought:

Read 6 books from one genre.

Today:

I have my craft.

Prompt:

Describe the light through the window.

April 20

What is more important in a library than anything else = than
everything else – is that fact that it exists.
~ Archibald MacLeish

Thought:

Double-check technical terms.

Today:

The better my focus is the better my writing.

Prompt:

Describe the dark.

April 21

I think it's bad to talk about one's present work, for it spoils something at the root of the creative act. It discharges the tension.

~ Norman Mailer

Thought:

Have a friend read your piece aloud.

Today:

I will note all the seeds of new stories in my life.

Prompt:

List 3 ways to smile.

April 22

The cure for boredom is curiosity. There is no sure
for curiosity.
~ Dorothy Parker

Thought:

Taste something new.

Today:

I will accept direction from the editor.

Prompt:

Describe a wooden chair.

April 23

Some books are to tasted, others to be swallowed, and a few to
be chewed and digested: that is, some books are to be read
only in parts, others to be read, but not curiously and some
few to be read wholly, and with diligence and attention.
~ Sir Francis Bacon

Thought:

Allow the manuscript time to rest before the final edit.

Today:

I will trust my instincts.

Prompt:

Describe 3 reasons to laugh.

April 24

Nothing is stronger than habit.
                    ~ Ovid

Thought:

What makes a successful transition?

Today:

I will interview an interesting person.

Prompt:

Describe a funeral.

April 25

A writer's mind seems to be situated partly in solar plexus
and partly in the head.

~ Ethel Wilson

Thought:

Guidelines = Format

Today:

I will think clearly.

Prompt:

Describe an exotic place.

April 26

I am a part of all I have read.
                              ~ John Kieran

Thought:

Write short essays on favorite subjects.

Today:

I will remember a positive outcome is as likely as a negative one.

Prompt:

Describe a cat.

April 27

Be obscure clearly.

~ E.B. White

Thought:

Proofread your letters.

Today:

I will not think of old reflections that drag me down: onward and forward.

Prompt:

List 3 colors of sad.

April 28

Do not turn back when you are just at the goal.
~ Publilis Syrus

Thought:

Write a query to an agent.

Today:

I understand my feelings are not right or wrong.

Prompt:

Write a song.

April 29

All great truths begin as blasphemies.
~ George Bernard Shaw

Thought:

As the character: what's important?

Today:

I acknowledge my mistakes and correct them.

Prompt:

Describe a newspaper.

April 30

Learn to write well, or not to write at all.
                          ~ John Sheffield

Thought:

Volunteer in the community.

Today:

I will call my mentor and touch base.

Prompt:

Describe the speed of light.

May 1

Drama, instead of telling us the whole of a man's life, must place him in such a situation; tie such a knot, that when it is untied, the whole man is visible.

~ Leo Tolstoy

Thought:

The perfect sentence: write it down.

Today:

I will complete my thought.

Prompt:

Write a paragraph about wind.

May 2

What no wife of a writer can ever understand is that the writer is working when he's staring out the window.
~ Burton Rascoe

Thought:

Take notes.

Today:

I will take care of my own business.

Prompt:

List 5 colors of joy.

May 3

I will not add another word.
>   ~ Horace

Thought:

Action, action, action...

Today:

I will balance the day.

Prompt:

List 5 ways to light a candle.

May 4

Faith is taking the first step, even when you don't see the whole staircase.
> ~ Martin Luther King, Jr.

Thought:

Write character sketches.

Today:

I will support another writer with a purchase of a new genre selection.

Prompt:

Describe 3 noses.

May 5

To me, the greatest pleasure of writing is not what it's about, but the inner music the words make.
~ Truman Capote

Thought:

Identify your goals.

Today:

I will burn a rejection letter and let it go.

Prompt:

Describe chili hot.

May 6

There is something delicious about writing the first words of a story. You never quite know where they'll take you.
~ Beatrix Potter

Thought:

Create a world with words.

Today:

I will progress on one project.

Prompt:

Explain Money.

May 7

Anyone could write a novel, given six weeks, pen, paper and
no telephone or wife.
~ Evelyn Waugh

Thought:

Sacrifice moves people.

Today:

I will share my last essay/chapter with another writer.

Prompt:

Describe the curtains.

May 8

It takes a long time to publish a book.
                              ~ Kenneth Koch

Thought:

Story begins: 1st problem, 2nd problem, 3rd problem, climax and resolution.

Today:

I will be pleasant to my editor.

Prompt:

Describe a dog.

May 9

Experience is the name everyone gives to their mistakes.
~ Oscar Wilde

Thought:

Create a couple with true love.

Today:

I will remember to eat, drink and be merry.

Prompt:

List 3 people of consequence.

May 10

Writing is the hardest way of earning a living, with the
possible exception of wrestling alligators.
~ William Saroyan

Thought:

Read 3 books from each publisher you query.

Today:

I will improve my vocabulary.

Prompt:

List 10 classes from middle school / junior high school.

May 11

I must write it all out, at any cost. Writing is thinking. It is more than living, for it is being conscious of living.
~ Anne Morrow Lindberg

Thought:

Edit for unnecessary words.

Today:

I will add conflict to my plot.

Prompt:

Describe the book shelf.

May 12

Most people are unable to write because they are unable to think, and they are unable to think because they congenially lack the equipment to do so, just as they congenially lack the equipment to fly over the moon.

~ Henry Louis Mencken

Thought:

Create a story board.

Today:

I will take my anger out on a character in my story.

Prompt:

Describe the hall.

May 13

If indeed you must be candid, be candid beautifully.
~ Kahlil Gibran

Thought:

Writers have a tool box. What's in yours?

Today:

I will practice my craft.

Prompt:

List 5 words for smooth.

May 14

Writing is learning to say nothing, more cleverly each day.
~ William Allingham

Thought:

Ability, facility, humility, gentility

Today:

I will remember where I begin.

Prompt:

Describe her shoes.

May 15

To finish is a sadness to a writer – a little death. He puts the last word down and it is done. But it isn't really done. The story goes on and leaves the writer behind, for no story is ever done.

~ John Steinbeck

Thought:

Humor temporarily relieves tension.

Today:

I will tell a story.

Prompt:

List 5 colors of leaves.

May 16

There are men that will make you books, and turn them loose into the world, with as much dispatch as they would do a dish of fritters.

~ Miguel de Cervantes

Thought:

Romance is suspense.

Today:

I will not blame others for my procrastination.

Prompt:

Describe the scent of ink.

May 17

Books are funny little portable pieces of thought.
~ Susan Sontag

Thought:

Write a journal entry.

Today:

I will celebrate my accomplishments.

Prompt:

Describe a fair.

May 18

Thank goodness I was never sent to school; it would have rubbed off some of the originality.
                    ~ Beatrix Potter

Thought:

Write tight.

Today:

I will think, write, create, and hope.

Prompt:

Describe the reason for the fight.

May 19

It is the mark of an educated mind to entertain an idea
without accepting it.

~ Aristotle

Thought:

There needs to be tension between characters.

Today:

I will enjoy my choices.

Prompt:

Describe warmth of a muffin.

May 20

Courage is resistance to fear, mastery of fear – not absence of fear.

~ Mark Twain

Thought:

Wander Aimlessly.

Today:

I will learn from today's experiences.

Prompt:

Write a paragraph about the mayor.

May 21

A moment's thinking is an hour in words.
~ Thomas Hood

Thought:

Outline Historical Fiction.

Today:

I will focus on this project.

Prompt:

Describe a garden.

May 22

The most essential gift for a good writer is a built-in, shockproof shit detector. This is the writer's radar and all great writers have had it.

~ Ernest Hemingway

Thought:

Attend a writing workshop.

Today:

I will make a positive change.

Prompt:

List 5 reasons to lie.

May 23

Knowledge must come through action; you can have no test
which is not fanciful, save by trial.
~ Sophocles

Thought:

Create a system for completion.

Today:

I will not lose sight of my goal.

Prompt:

Think Red... Write it...

May 24

No one can write decently who is distrustful of the reader's intelligence or whose attitude is patronizing.
~ E.B. White

Thought:

How does the character walk?

Today:

I will keep an open mind to criticism.

Prompt:

Describe the smells of a train station.

May 25

The beginning is the most important part of the work.
~ Plato

Thought:

Avoid rushing the ending.

Today:

I will build on a foundation.

Prompt:

Think Silver... Write it...

May 26

When I was about eight, I decided that the most wonderful
thing, next to a human being, was a book.
~ Margaret Walker

Thought:

Edit for inconsistency in the story.

Today:

I will seek other writers who also need break time.

Prompt:

List 5 qualities of home.

May 27

Writing is not a profession but a vocation of unhappiness.
~ George Simenon

Thought:

Plot, Dialogue, Characterization

Today:

I will reassess my priorities.

Prompt:

Describe the sky.

May 28

Style is the perfection of a point of view.
                    ~ Richard Eberhart

Thought:

Omniscient point of view gets into the character's thoughts.

Today:

I will take a step back to look at my progress.

Prompt:

Describe the inside of a bank.

May 29

So the writer who breeds more words than he needs is making
a chore for those who read.
~ Theodor Seuss Geisel

Thought:

Of what importance are first impressions?

Today:

I will not limit my ideas but take notes.

Prompt:

Describe the feeling of sick.

May 30

Books are the carriers of civilization. Without books, history is silent, literature dumb, science crippled, thought and speculation at a standstill.
~ Henry David Thoreau

Thought:

Choose vivid words.

Today:

I will clear my calendar of non-productive activity.

Prompt:

Describe the sound of a train.

May 31

The best time for planning a book is while you're doing the dishes.
                              ~ Agatha Christie

Thought:

Simplify the scene.

Today:

I will reveal myself in my writing.

Prompt:

Describe a reason for murder.

June 1

My purpose is to entertain myself first and other
people secondly.

> ~ John D. MacDonald

Thought:

Edit for redundant words.

Today:

I will toast my new project.

Prompt:

List 7 ways to stir a pot.

June 2

When I used to teach creative writing, I would tell the students to make their characters want something right away even if it's only a glass of water. Characters paralyzed by the meaninglessness of modern life still have to drink water from time to time.

~ Kurt Vonnegut

Thought:

Describe the smell.

Today:

I will not be stuck in an old unproductive pattern.

Prompt:

Describe a voodoo priestess.

June 3

I can't write five words but that I change seven.
~ Dorothy Parker

Thought:

Attend a conference.

Today:

I will format the scene.

Prompt:

Describe the flag.

June 4

You see things; and say 'Why?' But I dream things that never were and say, "Why not?'
~ George Bernard Shaw

Thought:

Read the newspaper.

Today:

I will put more emotion in my writing.

Prompt:

Describe a pillow.

June 5

Be generous, be delicate, and always pursue the prize.
~ Henry James

Thought:

Outline a science fiction story.

Today:

I will improve my grammar.

Prompt:

Describe finding a treasure.

June 6

Give me books, fruit, French wine and fine weather and a little
music out of doors, play by somebody I do not know.
~ John Keats

Thought:

Write about fear.

Today:

I will develop a new character.

Prompt:

Describe twins.

June 7

We do not write in order to be understood; we write in order to understand.

~ C. Day Lewis

Thought:

Who is the audience?

Today:

I will outline the next 3 steps of my project.

Prompt:

Think Brown… Write it…

June 8

The two most engaging powers of an author are to make new things familiar and familiar things new.
~ Samuel Johnson

Thought:

Develop the skill to write concisely.

Today:

I will write.

Prompt:

Think Orange... Write it...

June 9

If any man wish to write in a clear style let him first be clear in his thoughts; and if any would write in a noble style, let him possess a noble soul.
                    ~ Johann Wolfgang von Goethe

Thought:

Edit for consistency of character thought and action.

Today:

I will practice dialogue.

Prompt:

Describe the enemy.

June 10

A coward turns away, but a brave man's choice is danger.
~ Euripides

Thought:

Think it through to the end.

Today:

I will develop a new skill.

Prompt:

Describe the crunch.

June 11

You must be the change you want to see in the world.
~ Mahatma Ghandi

Thought:

Edit between submissions.

Today:

I will interview a new contact for future research.

Prompt:

Describe the last day of school.

June 12

There is no such thing as a moral or immoral book. Books are well written or badly written.
~ Oscar Wilde

Thought:

Research eras in history

Today:

I will de-clutter my area.

Prompt:

Describe a boat.

June 13

The work never matches the dream of perfection the artist has to start with.
                    ~ William Faulkner

Thought:

Develop a plan.

Today:

I will write to one agent.

Prompt:

Describe a dream.

June 14

Only a person with a best seller mind can write a Best Seller.
~ Aldous Huxley

Thought:

Research

Today:

I will express love.

Prompt:

Describe a safe place.

June 15

We are what we repeatedly do. Excellence then, is not an act, but a habit.
~ Aristotle

Thought:

Would your character know all the details?

Today:

I will focus on the next step.

Prompt:

Describe the sign.

June 16

When someone does something good, Applaud! You make
two people happy.
~ Samuel Goldwyn

Thought:

Sample chapters should be of the same quality as the rest of
the book.

Today:

I will notice the details of a new location; store, or restaurant.

Prompt:

Describe laughing.

June 17

The role of a writer is not to say what we all can say, but what we are unable to.

~ Anais Nin

Thought:

Be specific.

Today:

I will write to the editor-in-chief.

Prompt:

Describe a glass of wine.

June 18

Not that the story need be long, but it will take a long while to make it short.

~ Henry David Thoreau

Thought:

Read a book by an expert.

Today:

I will write something magical.

Prompt:

List 3 smells of a classroom.

June 19

We learn from failure not from success.
                              ~ Bram Stoker

Thought:

Who, what, where, when, why

Today:

I will be patient with myself.

Prompt:

List 5 character defects exhibited by your hero.

June 20

Three hours a day will produce as much as a man ought to write.

~ Anthony Trollope

Thought:

Design a character family tree.

Today:

I will re-write a weak paragraph.

Prompt:

Describe a romantic dinner.

June 21

Nurture your mind with great thoughts; to believe in the heroic makes heroes.
~ Benjamin Disraeli

Thought:

Write one page scene.

Today:

I will move forward.

Prompt:

Describe a candy shop.

June 22

The life of the creative man is lead, directed and controlled by boredom. Avoiding boredom is one of our most important purposes.

~ Susan Sontag

Thought:

Complete your sentence.

Today:

I will accept, suggest and try new solutions.

Prompt:

List 3 ways to drive a car.

June 23

Look with favor upon a bold beginning.
                    ~ Virgil

Thought:

Practice paragraphs.

Today:

I will be responsible for myself.

Prompt:

List 3 reasons to join a party.

June 24

Once writing has become your major vice and greatest pleasure, only death can stop it.
~ Ernest Hemingway

Thought:

What is the purpose of a dictionary? How do I use it?

Today:

I will acknowledge my level of self-discipline.

Prompt:

Describe a dirty dish.

June 25

If you ask me what I came to do in this world, I, an artist, will answer you: I am here to live out loud.
~ Emile Zola

Thought:

Develop a group of writer friends.

Today:

I will change my process.

Prompt:

Describe a giant.

June 26

Reading makes a full man, conference a ready man, writing an exact man.

~ Sir Francis Bacon

Thought:

Poor grammar is distracting.

Today:

I will close the door and turn off the phone for one hour.

Prompt:

Describe the dress she wore the day they met.

June 27

If you are going to make a book end badly, it must end badly from the beginning.
                    ~ Robert Louis Stevenson

Thought:

Revise character voice to fit the character.

Today:

I will provide a new solution to a dilemma.

Prompt:

Describe a summer day.

June 28

He who never hoped can never despair.
~ George Bernard Shaw

Thought:

Check point of view.

Today:

I will write in a new location.

Prompt:

Think Green... Write it...

June 29

What a blessed thing it is that nature, when she invented,
manufactured and patented her authors, contrived to make
critics out of the chips that were left!
~ Oliver Wendell Holmes

Thought:

What does she have in her purse?

Today:

I will not divert from my primary aim.

Prompt:

Describe Ice Cream.

June 30

I fear those big words which make us so unhappy.
~ James Joyce

Thought:

Consider advice from editors. Disregard form letters.

Today:

I will consider a partner to balance my deficiencies.

Prompt:

List 3 ways to follow a clue.

July 1

By writing much, one learns to write well.
~ Robert Southey

Thought:

Outline a museum book.

Today:

I will listen for new information.

Prompt:

List 3 reasons to sing.

July 2

You must keep sending work out; you must never let a
manuscript do nothing but eat its head off in a drawer. You
send that work out again and again, while you're working on
another one. If you have talent, you will receive some measure
of success – but only if you persist.

~ Isaac Asimov

Thought:

What is the purpose of a thesaurus? How do I use it?

Today:

I will submit a non-fiction article.

Prompt:

Describe the scent of bread.

July 3

All our dreams can come true, if we have the courage to
pursue them.

~ Walt Disney

Thought:

Move from problem to solution.

Today:

I will mentor another writer. Helping another may help me.

Prompt:

Describe the church.

July 4

Editor: A person employed by a newspaper, whose business it is to separate the wheat from the chaff, and to see that the chaff is printed.
~ Elbert Hubbard

Thought:

Take notes everywhere.

Today:

I will write from a different perspective.

Prompt:

Describe an elf.

July 5

Writing a book is horrible, exhausting struggle, like a long bout of some painful illness. One would never undertake such things if one were not driven on by some demon whom one can neither resist nor understand.
~ George Orwell

Thought:

Write a one page conversation.

Today:

I will take a step forward.

Prompt:

Describe grandma's rocker.

July 6

Wear an old coat and buy a new book.
                                    ~ Austin Phelps

Thought:

Cut Cliché.

Today:

I will work on my project.

Prompt:

Describe a click.

July 7

The only reason for being a professional writer is that you just can't help it.

~ Leo Rosten

Thought:

Write a surprise.

Today:

I will contribute to a support group.

Prompt:

Describe floating.

July 8

Every writer I know has trouble writing.
~ Joseph Heller

Thought:

Is the dialogue believable?

Today:

I will constructively comment on a piece I enjoyed reading.

Prompt:

Describe the color of hate.

July 9

Publication – is the auction of the Mind of Man.
~ Emily Dickinson

Thought:

Create a submission package.

Today:

I will follow my instinct.

Prompt:

Describe popcorn.

July 10

For several days after my first book was published, I carried it about in my pocket and took surreptitious peeps at it to make sure the ink had not faded.
~ Sir James Matthew Barrie

Thought:

Read about writing.

Today:

I will enjoy life.

Prompt:

Describe how a thorn feels.

July 11

A room without books is like a body without a soul.
~ Marcus Cicero

Thought:

Choose a normal word.

Today:

I will find a friend who will ask about my progress in one month's time.

Prompt:

Describe a legacy.

July 12

A journey of a thousand miles begins with a single step.
~ Lao-tse

Thought:

Set goals.

Today:

I will nurture my talent.

Prompt:

Describe an argument.

July 13

You write that first draft really to see how it's going to come out.

~ James A. Michener

Thought:

The first chapter needs a hook.

Today:

I will replace negative with positive.

Prompt:

Describe the smell of money.

July 14

The only way to write is to write.
~ Peggy Teeters

Thought:

Complete a crossword puzzle.

Today:

I will examine my progress and give myself an honest assessment.

Prompt:

Describe your favorite pen.

July 15

I demand that my books be judged with utmost severity, by
knowledgeable people who know the rules of grammar and of
logic, and who will seek beneath the footsteps of my commas,
the lice of my thought in the head of my style.
~ Louis Aragon

Thought:

What is your favorite word? Why?

Today:

I will focus on one paragraph at a time.

Prompt:

Write two lines about insects.

July 16

For a creative writer possession of the "truth" is less important than emotional sincerity.
~ George Orwell

Thought:

Write until you find your voice.

Today:

I will trust the voices in my head to write a good story.

Prompt:

Describe happily ever after.

July 17

I'm not doing this for the money. I'm doing it because it needs to be done.
~ Eric Knight

Thought:

Ignore writer's block.

Today:

I will relax and dream dreams.

Prompt:

Describe the pages of a book.

July 18

I want to write books that unlock the traffic jam in everybody's head.
                    ~ John Updike

Thought:

Anagram for Phantom

Today:

I will add deadlines to my calendar.

Prompt:

Write 5 words in alphabetical order.

July 19

The best style is the style you don't notice.
                    ~ W. Somerset Maugham

Thought:

Is love a significant element?

Today:

I will use my imagination.

Prompt:

List 10 items on a menu.

July 20

If I don't write to empty my mind, I go mad.
~ Lord Byron

Thought:

Write a journal page as a character in the first person.

Today:

I will change perspective.

Prompt:

Describe a tall man.

July 21

I never started from ideas but always from character.
~ Ivan Turgenev

Thought:

Read like a writer.

Today:

I will subscribe to a publication that pays writers for their work.

Prompt:

Describe a factory.

July 22

Never promise more than you can perform.
~ Publilis Syrus

Thought:

Check word choice.

Today:

I will acknowledge experience is my teacher.

Prompt:

List 3 virtues.

July 23

The fact that I have been successful merely means that I can write and illustrate in my own way.
~ Hugh Lofting

Thought:

Make a list of prospective agents.

Today:

I will write with enthusiasm.

Prompt:

Describe a ghost.

July 24

It should be our care not to live a long life as a
satisfactory one.

~ Seneca

Thought:

Describe how the characters meet.

Today:

I will ask for help.

Prompt:

List 3 shades of pink.

July 25

A real book is not one that we read, but one that reads us.
~ W. H. Auden

Thought:

Make your deadlines.

Today:

I will start fresh.

Prompt:

Describe a gasp.

July 26

You may delay but time will not.
                    ~ Benjamin Franklin

Thought:

Explain the complicated.

Today:

I will turn the page on procrastination.

Prompt:

Describe ice.

July 27

One of the advantages of being disorderly is that one is constantly making exciting discoveries.
                              ~ A.A. Milne

Thought:

Follow submission guidelines.

Today:

I will enter a contest.

Prompt:

List 3 reasons to shoot a gun.

July 28

The historian records, but the novelist creates.
~ E.M. Forster

Thought:

Start with a feeling.

Today:

I will set boundaries.

Prompt:

List 10 soft things.

July 29

Be not simply good; be good for something.
~ Henry David Thoreau

Thought:

Write what you know.

Today:

I will not be afraid to follow the truth where it leads.

Prompt:

Describe a bear.

July 30

It does not matter how slowly you go so long as you do
not stop.
~ Confucius

Thought:

Understand each sentence.

Today:

I will be a writer who writes.

Prompt:

Describe the taste of fries.

July 31

Never take the advice of someone who has not had your kind
of trouble.
~ Sydney J. Harris

Thought:

Seek ideas.

Today:

I will begin.

Prompt:

List 5 ways to dance.

August 1

I have long felt that any reviewer who expresses rage and loathing for a novel is preposterous. He or she is like a person who has put on full armor and attacked a hot fudge sundae or banana split.
~ Kurt Vonnegut

Thought:

Compassion creates understanding.

Today:

I will write about sorrows in life.

Prompt:

Write a letter to an agent.

August 2

The only stupid thing about words is the spelling of them.
~ Laura Ingalls Wilder

Thought:

Outline a "How-to."

Today:

I will learn something new.

Prompt:

Describe the feeling of sand.

August 3

The misuse of language induces evil in the soul.
~ Socrates

Thought:

What does your character want?

Today:

I will overcome a block.

Prompt:

Describe a bar.

August 4

No one can speak well unless he thoroughly knows
his subject.
                            ~ Cicero

Thought:

Guilt motivates characters.

Today:

I will write about new beginnings.

Prompt:

Describe a feather.

August 5

Writing is a way of talking without being interrupted.
~ Jules Renard

Thought:

Does each character have a different voice, emotions and motivation?

Today:

I will write my story.

Prompt:

Describe lace.

August 6

Once we have accepted the story we cannot escape the
story's fate.
                    ~ Pamela Travers

Thought:

Edit background exposition.

Today:

I will twist the plot.

Prompt:

Describe bad breath.

August 7

The best way to get acquainted with a subject is to write a book about it.
                        ~ Benjamin Disraeli

Thought:

Increase the pace.

Today:

I appreciate my skills of communication.

Prompt:

Describe an angel.

August 8

To perceive is to suffer.

~ Aristotle

Thought:

Submit only your best.

Today:

I will go out with other writers & friends.

Prompt:

List 5 ways to feel good.

August 9

Write quickly and you will write well; write well, and you will soon write quickly.
~ Marcus Fabius Quintilianus

Thought:

Write two endings.

Today:

I will stick with the plan.

Prompt:

Describe an investigation.

August 10

The man who writes about himself and his own time is the only man who writes about all people and all time.
~ George Bernard Shaw

Thought:

Write a scene from a child's perspective.

Today:

I will aim for the right sentence or paragraph rather than the whole book.

Prompt:

Describe a yawn.

August 11

We are the music makers. We are the dreamers of the dream.
~ Arthur O'Shaughnessy

Thought:

Edit "that."

Today:

I will expand my understanding of culture.

Prompt:

Describe a breeze.

August 12

There's nothing to writing. All you do is sit down at a
typewriter and open a vein.
                    ~ Walter Wellesley "Red" Smith

Thought:

50% - 70% of popular fiction is dialogue.

Today:

I will meet my responsibilities.

Prompt:

Describe a mountain.

August 13

Writers should be read, but neither seen nor heard.
~ Daphne du Maurier

Thought:

Edit the lovely passages.

Today:

I will tell a story of heart break.

Prompt:

Describe an accent.

August 14

I get up in the morning, torture a typewriter until it screams, then stop.
~ Clarence Budington Kelland

Thought:

Research the details of an occupation.

Today:

I will focus my attention on my progress.

Prompt:

Explain a mystery.

August 15

Literature is a luxury; fiction is a necessity.
~ G.K. Chesterton

Thought:

Define the story and stick to it.

Today:

I will write about women.

Prompt:

Describe funky.

August 16

It is personalities not principles that move the age.
~ Oscar Wilde

Thought:

Create a special notebook of phrases.

Today:

I will not feel guilty. I will just get to work.

Prompt:

Describe a foot.

August 17

Self-confidence is the first requisite to great undertakings.
~ Samuel Johnson

Thought:

Avoid lengthy monologues or confessions.

Today:

I will quietly improve my piece of work.

Prompt:

Describe the feeling of compassion.

August 18

People ask for criticism, but they only want praise.
~ W. Somerset Maugham

Thought:

Use powerful verbs.

Today:

I will meet someone new.

Prompt:

Describe a goat.

August 19

Writing is a dog's life, but the only one worth living.
~ Gustave Flaubert

Thought:

Does my character evoke emotion?

Today:

I will discover an option.

Prompt:

Describe the candle light.

August 20

Writing is a form of therapy; sometimes I wonder how all those, who do not write, compose, or paint can manage to escape the madness, the melancholia, the panic fear, which is inherent in a human condition.
~ Graham Greene

Thought:

Secrets move the plot.

Today:

I will create a villain I love to hate.

Prompt:

Describe a jingle.

August 21

The writer has to force himself to work. He has to make his own hours and if he doesn't go to his desk at all there is nobody to scold him.

~ Roald Dahl

Thought:

Describe mannerisms.

Today:

I will schedule writing time.

Prompt:

Describe salvation.

August 22

If more of us valued food and cheer and song above hoarded gold, it would be a merrier world.
                    ~ J.R.R. Tolkien

Thought:

Notice the small stuff.

Today:

I will list what I want from writing.

Prompt:

Think Gray... Write it...

August 23

Where large sums of money are concerned, it is advisable to trust nobody.

~ Agatha Christie

Thought:

Edit warm up writing.

Today:

I will stop and smell the flowers.

Prompt:

List 5 attitudes of a bad person.

August 24

Exchange is creation.
                    ~ Muriel Rukeyser

Thought:

Edit useless information.

Today:

I will clear my mind of distractions.

Prompt:

Describe the way he walks.

August 25

My idea of a writer: someone interested in everything.
~ Susan Sontag

Thought:

Plan the confrontation.

Today:

I will work on my C.V. noting the body of work I've
completed.

Prompt:

Describe winter.

August 26

Education is the ability to listen to almost anything without losing your temper or your self-confidence.
                              ~ Robert Frost

Thought:

Edit for sentence structure.

Today:

I will change my attitude.

Prompt:

Describe a forest.

August 27

Whatever you can do or dream, begin it.
                    ~ Johann Wolfgang von Goethe

Thought:

Write 30 minutes per day. No matter what!

Today:

I will push myself to be better.

Prompt:

Describe decorations.

August 28

No one means all he says, and yet very few say all they mean,
for words are slippery and thought is viscous.
~ Henry Brooks Adams

Thought:

Why is that word there?

Today:

I will not cling to bad habits.

Prompt:

Describe breakfast.

August 29

Organizing is what you do before you do something, so that when you do it, it is not all mixed up.
~ A.A. Milne

Thought:

Read one related magazine per week.

Today:

I will make choices.

Prompt:

Describe a basket.

August 30

As was his language so was his life.
                        ~ Seneca

Thought:

What is the outcome of the scene?

Today:

I will write about beauty.

Prompt:

Describe a city block.

August 31

Wisdom outweighs wealth.
                    ~ Sophocles

Thought:

How do excellent writers craft scenes with dialogue.

Today:

I will write about alternatives.

Prompt:

Explain why she kissed the frog.

September 1

The reasonable man adapts himself to the world; the unreasonable one persists in trying to adapt the world to himself. Therefore, all progress depends upon the unreasonable man.

~ George Bernard Shaw

Thought:

Use the proper word.

Today:

I will be inspired to write.

Prompt:

Explain a joke.

September 2

Writing is its own reward.
                    ~ Henry Miller

Thought:

What makes a classic story?

Today:

I will learn a foreign word.

Prompt:

Describe a cane.

September 3

Nothing can be done at once hastily and prudently.
~ Publilis Syrus

Thought:

Bad guys aren't all bad.

Today:

I will make a point.

Prompt:

Describe a mouse.

September 4

Honest criticism is hard to take, particularly from a relative, a friend, an acquaintance, or a stranger.
~ Franklin Jones

Thought:

Is the character essential?

Today:

I will follow my dreams.

Prompt:

Describe Adventure.

September 5

The most valuable of all talents is that of never using two
words when one will do.
~ Thomas Jefferson

Thought:

Create a dialogue between a parent & child.

Today:

I will shut out criticism.

Prompt:

Describe a holy man.

September 6

I am never afraid of what I know.
~ Anna Sewell

Thought:

Edit adjectives.

Today:

I will research a local hero.

Prompt:

List 3 feelings.

September 7

Suspense: the only literary toll that has any effect upon tyrants and savages.

~ E.M. Forster

Thought:

Is there enough conflict to sustain the length of the book?

Today:

I will take responsibility for completing my project.

Prompt:

List 7 deadly sins.

September 8

It is dangerous to be right when the government is wrong.
~ Voltaire

Thought:

Heroes make mistakes.

Today:

I will write about a relationship.

Prompt:

Describe clean clothes.

September 9

I write as straight as I can, just as I walk as straight as I can,
because that is the best way to get there.
~ H. G. Wells

Thought:

Spend time with friends.

Today:

I will notice something new.

Prompt:

Describe humanity to a cow.

September 10

I love deadlines and the whooshing sound they make as they pass by.
~ Douglas Adams

Thought:

Read 3 versions of the same story.

Today:

I will be curious & write about it.

Prompt:

Describe a knight.

September 11

Times are bad. Children no longer obey their parents and everyone is writing a book.
                              ~ Cicero

Thought:

What is the character's religion or belief structure?

Today:

I will write a logical argument.

Prompt:

List military ranks.

September 12

Imagination is the beginning of creation. You imagine what you desire, you will what you imagine and at last you create what you will.

~ George Bernard Shaw

Thought:

Edit weak elements.

Today:

I will improve the dialogue.

Prompt:

Describe a cottage.

September 13

I am writing in the garden. To write as one should of a garden one must write not outside it or merely somewhere near it, but in the garden.

~ Frances Hodgson Burnett

Thought:

Be passionate.

Today:

I will buy a book.

Prompt:

Describe a pot.

September 14

The greatest good you can do for another is not just share
your riches, but to reveal to him his own.
                    ~ Benjamin Disraeli

Thought:

Is the character memorable?

Today:

I will write about something familiar.

Prompt:

List 10 stores at the mall.

September 15

Impatience is the mark of independence, not of bondage.
~ Marianne Moore

Thought:

Too many words, edit.

Today:

I will write with clarity.

Prompt:

Describe an alien.

September 16

Everywhere I go I'm asked if I think the university stifles
writers. My opinion is that they don't stifle enough of them.
There's many a bestseller that could have been prevented by a
good teacher.

~ Flannery O'Connor

Thought:

Check for contradiction.

Today:

I will submit my writing to publishers.

Prompt:

List 5 beige things.

September 17

The life is so short, the crafts so long to learn.
~ Geoffrey Chaucer

Thought:

Complete a character sketch.

Today:

I will write a believable hero.

Prompt:

Describe a fire.

September 18

The art of writing is the art of applying the seat of the pants to the seat of the chair.
~ Mary Heaton Vorse

Thought:

Do I have a saleable story?

Today:

I will write a book review.

Prompt:

Count every stair to the top.

September 19

Write down the thoughts of the moment. Those that come
unsought for are commonly the most valuable.
~ Sir Francis Bacon

Thought:

Play Boggle

Today:

I will write about emotions.

Prompt:

List 10 toys.

September 20

No one is useless in this world who lightens the burdens of another.
~ Charles Dickens

Thought:

Read psychology books to understand character traits.

Today:

I will use a new word.

Prompt:

List 5 reasons to fly to the moon.

September 21

If you can't annoy somebody with what you write, I think there's little point in writing.
~ Kingsley Amis

Thought:

Outline a science book.

Today:

I will write something humorous.

Prompt:

Explain life in the ocean.

September 22

Books are only a shadow and life the real thing. I believe this as strongly as any belief I hold.

~ Esther Forbes

Thought:

Edit minor characters to minor roles.

Today:

I will read the news.

Prompt:

List 5 hard things.

September 23

Watch out when you're getting all you want, fattened hogs ain't in luck.

~ Joel Chandler Harris

Thought:

Go to the store.

Today:

I will write about a great restaurant.

Prompt:

Describe make-up.

September 24

The story...must be a conflict, and specifically, a conflict between the forces of good and evil within a single person.
~ Maxwell Anderson

Thought:

Outline a children's book.

Today:

I will write a letter of thanks.

Prompt:

Describe a country store.

September 25

There are no dull subjects. There are only dull writers.
~ Henry Louis Mencken

Thought:

Disgrace is powerful motivation.

Today:

I will check the pace of my piece.

Prompt:

List 3 sounds on a farm.

September 26

If you want to tell people the truth, make them laugh,
otherwise they'll kill you.

~ Oscar Wilde

Thought:

What are the minor conflicts?

Today:

I will set new goals or revise the old ones.

Prompt:

Explain transformation.

September 27

A man is original when he speaks the truth that has always
been known to all good men.

~ Patrick Kavanagh

Thought:

Mumbo Jumbo Gumbo

Today:

I will check off my to-do list.

Prompt:

Write a tragic moment.

September 28

Technique alone is never enough. You have to have passion.
Technique alone is just another embroidered potholder.
~ Raymond Chandler

Thought:

Create a title list.

Today:

I will write about family.

Prompt:

Write a book review.

September 29

Writing comes more easily if you have something to say.
~ Sholem Asch

Thought:

What prevents the character from achieving the goal?

Today:

If I'm late for a deadline I will recommit to the project.

Prompt:

Describe a sidewalk.

September 30

If you would not be forgotten as soon as you are dead and rotten, either write something worth reading or do things worth the writing.

~ Benjamin Franklin

Thought:

The story is in the details.

Today:

I will start again.

Prompt:

Describe the King's Robe.

October 1

No tears in the writer, no tears in the reader.
~ George Moore

Thought:

Edit characters who don't do the job.

Today:

I will read a new writer.

Prompt:

Describe pearls.

October 2

Being forced to work, and forced to do your best, will breed in you temperance and self-control, diligence and strength of will, cheerfulness and content, and a hundred virtues which the idle will never know.
~ Charles Kingsley

Thought:

Is your story melodramatic?

Today:

I will write an editorial review.

Prompt:

Describe buttons.

October 3

Life is more amusing than we thought.
                    ~ Andrew Lang

Thought:

Keep criticism in perspective.

Today:

I will write about making the impossible possible.

Prompt:

Describe a sock.

October 4

Life is either a daring adventure or nothing.
~ Helen Keller

Thought:

Ethnic foods bring spice to a story.

Today:

I will submit a piece of work to a new publication.

Prompt:

Describe jail.

October 5

You can never get a cup of tea large enough or a book long enough to suit me.

~ C.S. Lewis

Thought:

Include special events in the story.

Today:

I will make choices.

Prompt:

List 5 happy times.

October 6

He who can does. He who cannot, teaches. A short saying oft
contains much wisdom.
                              ~ Sophocles

Thought:

Devotion moves characters through dilemma.

Today:

I will seek out talented friends to challenge me.

Prompt:

List 5 different wallets.

October 7

I love writing. I love the swirl and swing of words as they tangle with human emotions.
~ James Michener

Thought:

Edit irrelevant out.

Today:

I will accept my situation today and move forward.

Prompt:

Think Aqua…Write it…

October 8

The maker of a sentence launches out into the infinite and
builds a road into chaos and old night, and is followed by
those who hear him with something of wild creative delight.
~ Ralph Waldo Emerson

Thought:

Think thoughts. Write them. Delete all but the best.

Today:

I will revise an old piece.

Prompt:

Describe northern winter.

October 9

Woe to him that reads but one book.
                              ~ George Herbert

Thought:

Lies move the plot.

Today:

I will give my writing my full attention.

Prompt:

Describe empty.

October 10

The measure of artistic merit is the length to which a writer is willing to go in following his own compulsions.
                              ~ John Updike

Thought:

Read the middle. Does it lag?

Today:

I will make changes.

Prompt:

Describe a raven.

October 11

Freedom is not worth having if it does not include the freedom to make mistakes.
~ Mahatma Ghandi

Thought:

All writing is not created equal.

Today:

I will read to someone today.

Prompt:

Describe a path.

October 12

Every quotation contributes something to the stability and enlargement of the language.
~ Samuel Johnson

Thought:

Read Junk Mail.

Today:

I will write a poem.

Prompt:

Describe an Amazon.

October 13

My relatives say that they are glad I'm rich, but that they simply cannot read me.
~ Kurt Vonnegut

Thought:

Query a publisher whose books you read.

Today:

I will say goodbye to distraction.

Prompt:

Describe Destiny.

October 14

Enjoy when you can, and endure when you must.
~ Johann Wolfgang von Goethe

Thought:

Virtues motivate the good.

Today:

I will turn the page and start fresh.

Prompt:

Describe a friend.

October 15

I love being a writer. What I can't stand is the paperwork.
~ Peter De Vries

Thought:

Expand the characters experience.

Today:

I will let go if people who keep me from writing.

Prompt:

Describe the sun.

October 16

Remarks are not literature.
                    ~ Gertrude Stein

Thought:

Does time and place change the story?

Today:

I will write a letter of condolence.

Prompt:

Describe bliss.

October 17

I was working on the proof of one of my poems all the morning and took out a comma. In the afternoon, I put it back in.

~ Oscar Wilde

Thought:

Find new words.

Today:

I will complete one goal.

Prompt:

Describe a ship.

October 18

I'd rather be caught holding up a bank than stealing so much as a two-word phrase from another writer.
~ Jack Smith

Thought:

Check facts.

Today:

I will be very creative.

Prompt:

List 10 names you love.

October 19

It usually takes more than three weeks to prepare a good impromptu speech.
~ Mark Twain

Thought:

Foreshadow important events.

Today:

I will celebrate the improvement in my writing.

Prompt:

List 5 things in a box.

October 20

Tomorrow is always fresh, with no mistakes in it.
~ Lucy Maude Montgomery

Thought:

Does the end meet expectations?

Today:

I will not be distracted.

Prompt:

Describe a horse.

October 21

The ancient Greek definition of happiness was the full use of your powers along lines of excellence.
~ John F. Kennedy

Thought:

Write, rewrite and rewrite again.

Today:

I will help a new writer.

Prompt:

List 5 foods you hate.

October 22

A book is never a masterpiece: it becomes one.
~ Carl Sandburg

Thought:

Grammar is important.

Today:

I will edit out the unnecessary.

Prompt:

Describe a pirate.

October 23

You can never learn less, you can always learn more.
~ R. Buckminster Fuller

Thought:

Character shame is a motivator.

Today:

I will take a long look at my writing.

Prompt:

Describe loyalty.

October 24

To me, freedom entitles you to do something, not to not do something.

~ Shel Silverstein

Thought:

Begin at the beginning.

Today:

I will find a good section & make it better.

Prompt:

Describe the rug.

October 25

Make it new.
~ Ezra Pound

Thought:

What do emotions mean to the character?

Today:

I will write a diary entry.

Prompt:

Describe a pharaoh.

October 26

Words are a lens to focus one's mind.

~ Ayn Rand

Thought:

What does the protagonist want?

Today:

I will find joy in writing.

Prompt:

Describe life in 2 sentences.

October 27

Keep away from people who try to belittle your ambitions.
Small people always do that, but the really great make you
feel that you, too, can become great.
~ Mark Twain

Thought:

Cowards cause problems.

Today:

I will edit.

Prompt:

Describe a magic potion.

October 28

A woman must have money and a room of her own if she is to write fiction.
~ Virginia Woolf

Thought:

Annotate the draft.

Today:

I will write one small passage toward a larger piece of work.

Prompt:

List 5 things a lawyer says.

October 29

I have noticed that when things happen in one's imaginings, they never happen in one's life.
                    ~ Dodie Smith

Thought:

List the reasons why.

Today:

I will write a critique.

Prompt:

Describe Odin.

October 30

Books, the children of the brain.
                    ~ Jonathan Swift

Thought:

How do they move from here to there?

Today:

I will pay attention to details.

Prompt:

Write 4 sentences using 10 words.

October 31

Pay no attention to what the critics say; no statue has ever been erected to a critic.
~ Jean Sibelius

Thought:

Write through a writer's block.

Today:

I will push through the fear.

Prompt:

Describe grief.

November 1

Don't get it right, just get it written.
~ James Thurber

Thought:

Who knows the secret?

Today:

I will relish a good point.

Prompt:

Describe selfishness.

November 2

If you want to find out what a writer really feels, look at his work. That's enough.
>   ~ Shel Silverstein

Thought:

Edit for details.

Today:

I will improve punctuation.

Prompt:

Describe Spring.

November 3

Do not go where a path may lead, go instead where there is no path and leave a trail.
~ Ralph Waldo Emerson

Thought:

Outline a recipe book.

Today:

I will be open to new ideas.

Prompt:

Write a letter to your favorite author.

November 4

Energy and persistence conquer all things.
~ Benjamin Disraeli

Thought:

Reread your favorite childhood book.

Today:

I will notice the brilliance of color.

Prompt:

List 3 reasons to stand in a line.

November 5

It does make a difference what you call things.
~ Kate D. Wiggin

Thought:

Recheck heavily rewritten passages,

Today:

I will study a new language.

Prompt:

Describe a secret.

November 6

All books are either dreams or swords. You can cut, or you can drug, with words.

~ Amy Lowell

Thought:

Traitors create conflict.

Today:

I will take another step toward my goal.

Prompt:

Describe an escalator.

November 7

The awful thing, a kid reading, was that you came to the end of the story, and that was it. I mean, it would be heartbreaking that there was no more of it.
~ Robert Creeley

Thought:

Show, don't tell.

Today:

I will read a new author.

Prompt:

Describe a lady.

November 8

There is no happiness in love except at the end of an
English novel.
~ Anthony Trollope

Thought:

Create a new world.

Today:

I will trust my instincts.

Prompt:

Write a thank you note to a waitress.

November 9

Genius is not a quality, but only a quantitative difference in a combination of attributes contained in all persons.
~ Dr. Ernest Jones

Thought:

Greed creates conflict.

Today:

I will walk in wonder.

Prompt:

List 5 reasons to go to war.

November 10

My aim is to put down what I see and what I feel in the best
and simplest way I can tell it.
                        ~ Ernest Hemingway

Thought:

Learn from mistakes.

Today:

I will direct my efforts.

Prompt:

Describe medicine.

November 11

After seven years of writing – and working many jobs to support my family – I finally got published.
~ Lloyd Alexander

Thought:

What is the major sound of conflict?

Today:

I will write a letter of recommendation for the character.

Prompt:

Describe the road home.

November 12

Do not hire a man who does your work for money, but him
who does it for love of it.

~ Henry David Thoreau

Thought:

Create a monster.

Today:

I will find a kindred spirit.

Prompt:

Write a poem about the sea.

November 13

Life itself is the most wonderful fairy tale.
                    ~ Hans Christian Andersen

Thought:

Is the character believable?

Today:

I will breathe deeply!

Prompt:

Describe your favorite shoes.

November 14

Our lives only improve when we take chances – and the
first and most difficult risk we can take is being honest
with ourselves.

~ Walter Anderson

Thought:

Describe the sounds.

Today:

I will remind myself of the reason I write.

Prompt:

List 5 ways to fall.

November 15

Character cannot be developed in ease and quiet. Only through experience of trial and suffering can the soul be strengthened, ambition inspired, and success achieved.
~ Helen Keller

Thought:

Write every day.

Today:

I will see things as they could be.

Prompt:

Describe old.

November 16

There is no mistaking a real book when one meets it. It is like falling in love.
> ~ Christopher Morley

Thought:

Read aloud.

Today:

I will explore a new philosophy or point of view.

Prompt:

Describe a detective.

November 17

To produce a mighty book, you must choose a mighty theme.
~ Herman Melville

Thought:

Character defects are motivators.

Today:

I will tie up loose ends.

Prompt:

Describe Justice.

November 18

Old myths, old gods, old heroes have never died. They are
only sleeping at the bottom of our mind, waiting for our call.
We have need for them. They represent the wisdom of
our race.

~ Stanley Kunitz

Thought:

Write your dreams.

Today:

I will be willing to face the truth.

Prompt:

Describe your favorite painting.

November 19

Words – so innocent and powerless as they are, as standing in a dictionary, how potent for good and evil they become in the hands of one who knows how to combine them.
~ Nathaniel Hawthorne

Thought:

Edit out the tedious.

Today:

I will write an obituary.

Prompt:

Describe balloons.

November 20

The road to ignorance is paved with good editors.
~ George Barnard Shaw

Thought:

Go to a restaurant.

Today:

I will research a new topic.

Prompt:

List 5 T.V. shows.

November 21

Children read books, not reviews. They don't give a hoot about critics.
~ Isaac Bashevis Singer

Thought:

What is s/he wearing?

Today:

I will think backwards.

Prompt:

Describe a prayer.

November 22

It is a bad plan that admits of no modification.
                    ~ Publilis Syrus

Thought:

Play scrabble

Today:

I will allow myself to get carried away.

Prompt:

Describe a building.

November 23

I'm a great believer in luck, I find the more I work the more I have of it.

~ Thomas Jefferson

Thought:

Edit adverbs

Today:

I will create 3 steps to a small goal.

Prompt:

Describe an eagle.

November 24

A writer is somebody for whom writing is more difficult than it is for other people.
~ Thomas Mann

Thought:

Describe what you must.

Today:

I will write a declaration of intent.

Prompt:

Describe the smell of a library.

November 25

I want to be able, as days go by, always to look myself straight in the eye.
~ Edgar Guest

Thought:

Write a great letter.

Today:

I will dismiss negativity.

Prompt:

Describe a banquet.

November 26

I'm not a very good writer, but I'm an excellent rewriter.
~ James Michener

Thought:

Write a letter to an editor.

Today:

I will place all experience into three categories: animal, vegetable, mineral.

Prompt:

Write a list of hair styles.

November 27

As to the adjective, when in doubt, strike it out.
~ Mark Twain

Thought:

Write 1,000 words.

Today:

I will see the good points.

Prompt:

Describe futility.

November 28

Wise men talk because they have something to say; fools talk because they have something to say.
~ Plato

Thought:

Outline an action book.

Today:

I will think fundamentally logically.

Prompt:

Describe a throne.

November 29

If one does not know to which port one is sailing, no wind is favorable.

~ Seneca

Thought:

Write a dialogue between an older character and a younger character.

Today:

I will laugh at the absurdity of life.

Prompt:

Describe fabric.

November 30

From now on, ending a sentence with a preposition is something up with which I will not put.
~ Winston Churchill

Thought:

Build a story.

Today:

I will try a new option.

Prompt:

Describe hope.

December 1

Great is the art of beginning, but greater is the art of ending.
~ Henry Wadsworth Longfellow

Thought:

Go to a grocery store.

Today:

I look forward to the day.

Prompt:

Write to the newspaper.

December 2

The best way to have a good idea is to have lots of ideas.
~ Linus Pauling

Thought:

Write about an everyday hero.

Today:

I will talk with someone new.

Prompt:

Describe a motorcycle.

December 3

The secret of success is the constancy of purpose.
~ Benjamin Disraeli

Thought:

Am I on schedule?

Today:

I will influence another person.

Prompt:

Describe the suburbs.

December 4

A writer is unfair to himself when he is unable to be hard
on himself.
~ Marianne Moore

Thought:

Is there balance of white space, dialogue and description?

Today:

I will write to the president.

Prompt:

Describe wood.

December 5

Many books require no thought from those who read them, and for a very simple reason: they make no such demand upon those who wrote them.

~ Charles Caleb Colton

Thought:

Read Letters.

Today:

I will grow in freedom.

Prompt:

Describe the sea shore.

December 6

Wheresoever you go, you go with all your heart.
~ Confucius

Thought:

Did it happen in your life?

Today:

I will write the truth.

Prompt:

Describe a wheelchair.

December 7

Beware lest you lose the substance by grabbing at the shadow.
~ Aesop

Thought:

Write real characters.

Today:

I will watch two people talk with each other.

Prompt:

Describe a desk.

December 8

We do not write because we want to; we write because we have to.
                    ~ W. Somerset Maugham

Thought:

Do what you can.

Today:

I will write a short story for the season.

Prompt:

Describe ducklings.

December 9

I declare of all things there is nothing more enjoyable
than reading!
~ Jane Austen

Thought:

Tell the story.

Today:

I will help someone with my positive attribute.

Prompt:

Describe a cabin.

December 10

Writing is both mask and unveiling.
                            ~ E.B. White

Thought:

Close your eyes, write what you see.

Today:

I will find joy in a small thing.

Prompt:

Describe a diner.

December 11

Little by little, one travels far.
~ J.R.R. Tolkien

Thought:

Write 500 words.

Today:

I will write something risky.

Prompt:

Describe a cigar.

December 12

A writer without interest or sympathy for the foibles of his
fellow man is not conceivable as a writer.
~ Joseph Conrad

Thought:

Tell the truth.

Today:

I will write dialogue.

Prompt:

Describe swords.

December 13

There's no money in poetry, but then there's no poetry in money either.

~ Robert Graves

Thought:

Envy creates conflict.

Today:

I will make a commitment.

Prompt:

Describe a stream.

December 14

The wisest men follow their own directions.
~ Euripides

Thought:

Writing equals tools plus thoughts.

Today:

I will refine my skills.

Prompt:

Describe a crime.

December 15

What is done let us leave alone.
                    ~ Publius Terentius Afer

Thought:

Love is the greatest motivation.

Today:

I will make progress in a tangible way.

Prompt:

Make a list of what is done. Make a list of what to do.

December 16

Always aim at complete harmony of thought, word and deed.
~ Mahatma Ghandi

Thought:

Deceit creates conflict.

Today:

I will take the path of least resistance.

Prompt:

Describe the middle.

December 17

Fiction is obliged to stick to the possibilities. Truth isn't.
~ Mark Twain

Thought:

It isn't always a happy ending.

Today:

I will cherish a moment and write about it.

Prompt:

List 5 reasons to start again.

December 18

Be true to your work, your word and your friend.
~ Henry David Thoreau

Thought:

Does each chapter tell a good story?

Today:

I will choose the day.

Prompt:

Describe a cafeteria.

December 19

Difficulties strengthen the mind, as labor does the body.
~ Seneca

Thought:

Outline a decade.

Today:

I will move in the right direction.

Prompt:

Describe soup.

December 20

Find out the reason that commands you to write; see whether
it has spread its roots into the very depth of your heart;
confess to yourself you would have to die if you were
forbidden to write.

~ Rainer Maria Rilke

Thought:

Write the scene from 3 perspectives.

Today:

I will take a moment to gather energy.

Prompt:

Describe an alley.

December 21

When a man is in doubt about this or that in his writing, it will often guide him if he asks himself how it will tell a hundred years hence.
                    ~ Samuel Butler

Thought:

Does the chapter end with a cliff hanger?

Today:

I will extend myself to love the unlovable and write about it.

Prompt:

Describe disgusting.

December 22

Quotation: The act of repeating erroneously the words
of another.
~ Ambrose Bierce

Thought:

Write post cards.

Today:

I will make a change for the better.

Prompt:

List 3 reasons to quit.

December 23

When you are right you cannot be too radical; when you are wrong you cannot be too conservative.
                    ~ Martin Luther King, Jr.

Thought:

Write clear sentences.

Today:

I will think about my secret dream.

Prompt:

List 5 birds.

December 24

Short words are best and old words are best of all.
~ Winston Churchill

Thought:

Edit adjectives.

Today:

I will finish the task I set for myself.

Prompt:

Describe an elephant.

December 25

Illusion is the first of all pleasures.
~ Oscar Wilde

Thought:

Gather stories everywhere.

Today:

I will not struggle.

Prompt:

List 7 weapons.

December 26

Sit down, and put down everything that comes into your head and then you're a writer. But an author is one who can judge his own stuff's worth, without pity, and destroy most of it.
~ Sidonie–Gabrielle Colette

Thought:

Editors don't know everything.

Today:

I will accept an invitation.

Prompt:

Describe bricks.

December 27

And as imagination bodies forth the forms of things
unknown, the poet's pen turns them into shapes, and gives to
airy nothings a local habitation and a name.
~ William Shakespeare

Thought:

Use the pace and cadence of the genre.

Today:

I will dream a dream.

Prompt:

Describe surprise.

December 28

There are two ways of speaking an audience will always like;
one is to tell them what they don't understand; and the other
it to tell them what they used to.
~ George Eliot

Thought:

Create reasonable timelines for the character progression.

Today:

I will work to overcome a difficulty.

Prompt:

Describe a foreign street.

December 29

It is impossible to discourage the real writers – they don't give
a damn what you say, they're going to write.
~ Sinclair Lewis

Thought:

Keep a diary.

Today:

I will move toward the target.

Prompt:

Describe paint.

December 30

No passion in the world is equal to the passion to alter someone else's draft.
                    ~ H. G. Wells

Thought:

Write a dialogue between lovers.

Today:

I will choose to think about the positive.

Prompt:

Describe a family tradition.

December 31

The process of writing has something infinite about it. Even though it is interrupted each night, it is one single notation.
~ Elias Canetti

Thought:

Love the words.

Today:

I will consider alternatives.

Prompt:

Write a letter of apology.

Quoted Authors

Acton, Harold Mario Mitchell Jul 5, 1904 – Feb 27, 1994
Adams, Douglas Mar 11, 1952 – May 11, 2001
Adams, Henry Brooks Feb 16, 1938 – Mar 27, 1918
Aesop 620 BC -564 BC
Afer, Publis Terentius 185 BC– 159 BC
Alcott, Louisa May Nov 29, 1832 – Mar 6, 1888
Alexander, Lloyd Jan 30, 1924 – May 17, 2007
Allingham, William Mar 19, 1824 – Nov 18, 1889
Amis, Kingsley Apr 16, 1922 – Oct 22, 1995
Andersen, Hans Christian Apr 2, 1805 – Aug 4, 1875
Anderson, Maxwell Dec 15, 1888 – Feb 28, 1959
Anderson, Walter Sep 29, 1903 – Nov 30, 1965
Aragon, Louis Oct 3, 1897 – Dec 24, 1982
Aristotle 384 BC- 322 BC
Asch, Sholem Nov 1, 1880 – Jul 10, 1957
Asimov, Isaac Jan 2, 1920 – Apr 6, 1992
Auden, W. H. Feb 21, 1907 – Sep 29, 1973
Austen, Jane Dec 16, 1775 – Jul 18, 1817
Bacon, Sir Francis Jan 22, 1561 – Apr 9, 1626
Barrie, James Matthew May 9, 1860 – Jun 19, 1937
Baum, L Frank May 15, 1856 – May 6, 1919
Bierce, Ambrose Jun 24, 1842 – 1913
Borges, Jorge Luis Aug 24, 1899 – Jun 14, 1986
Bowen, Catherine Drinker Jan 1, 1897 – Nov 1, 1973
Brodsky, Joseph May 24, 1940 – Jan 28, 1996
Breton, Andre Feb 19, 1896 – Sept 28, 1966
Bronte, Charlotte Apr 21, 1816 – Mar 30, 1855
Brooks, Van Wyck Feb 16, 1887 – May 2, 1963
Burnett, Frances Hodgson Nov 24, 1849 – Oct 29, 1924
Butler, Samuel Dec 4, 1835 – Jun 18, 1902
Byron, Lord George Gordon Jan 22, 1788 – Apr 19, 1824
Canetti, Elias Jul 25, 1905 – Aug 14, 1994
Capote, Truman Persons Sep 30, 1924 – Aug 25, 1984
Cervantes, Miguel Oct 9, 1547 – Apr 23, 1616

Chandler, Raymond Jul 23, 1888 – Mar 26, 1959
Chaucer, Geoffrey 1343 – Oct 25, 1400
Cheever, John May 27, 1912 – Jun 18, 1982
Checkov, Anton Jan 29, 1860 – Jul 15, 1904
Chesterton, G. K. May 29, 1874 – Jun 14, 1936
Christie, Dame Agatha Sept 15, 1890 – Jan 12, 1976
Churchill, Sir Winston Oct 26, 1951 – Apr 7, 1951
Cicero, Marcus Jan 3, 106 BC – Dec 7, 43 BC
Clampitt, Amy Jun 15, 1920 – Sep 10, 1994
Colette, Sidonie-Gabrielle Jan 28, 1873 – Aug 3, 1954
Colton, Charles Caleb 1780-1832
Confucius Sep 28, 551 BC – 479 BC
Connolly, Cyril Sep 10, 1903 – Nov 26, 1974
Conrad, Joseph Dec 3, 1857 – Aug 3, 1924
Creeley, Robert May 21, 1926 – Mar 30, 2005
cummings, e.e. Oct 14, 1894 – Sept 3, 1962
Dahl, Roald Sept 13, 1916 – Nov 25, 1990
De Vries, Peter Feb 27, 1910 – Sep 28, 1993
Dickens, Charles Feb 7, 1812 – Jun 9 1870
Dickenson, Emily Dec 10, 1830 – May 15, 1886
Disney, Walter Dec 5, 1901 – Dec 15, 1966
Disraeli, Benjamin Dec 21, 1804 – Apr 19, 1881
Drummond, Carlos Oct 31, 1902 – Aug 17, 1987
Eberhart, Richard Apr 5, 1904 – Jun 9, 2005
Eliot, George Nov 22, 1819 – Dec 22, 1880
Eliot, T.S. Sept 26, 1888 – Jan 4, 1965
Ellis, Havelock Feb 2, 1859 – Jul 8, 1939
Emerson, Ralph Waldo May 25, 1803 – Apr 27, 1882
Euripides 480 BC – 406 BC
Faulkner, William Sep 25, 1897 – Jul 6, 1962
Ferber, Edna Aug 15, 1885 – Apr 16, 1968
Fitzgerald, F. Scott Sep 24, 1896 – Dec 21, 1940
Flaubert, Gustave Dec 12, 1821 – May 8, 1880
Forbes, Esther Jun 28, 1891 – Aug 12, 1967
Forster, Edward Morgan Jan 1, 1879 - Jun 7, 1970
Fowler, Gene Mar 8, 1890 – Jul 2, 1960

Franklin, Benjamin Jan 17, 1706 – Apr 17, 1790
Frost, Robert Mar 26, 1874 – Jan 29, 1963
Fuller, Richard Buckminster Jul 12, 1895 – Jul 1 1983
Geisel, Theodor Seuss Mar2, 1904 – Sep 24, 1991
Ghandi, Mahatma Oct 2, 1869 – Jan 30, 1948
Gibran, Kahlil Jan6, 1883 – Apr 10, 1931
Gide, Andre Nov 22, 1869 – Feb 19, 1951
Goldwyn, Samuel Jul 1879 – Jan 31, 1974
Gracian, Baltazar Jan 8, 1601 – Dec 6, 1658
Graves, Robert Jul 24, 1895 – Dec 7, 1985
Greene, Henry Graham Oct 2, 1904 – Apr 3, 1991
Guest, Edgar Aug 20, 1881 – Aug 5, 1959
Hall, James Norman Apr 22, 1887 – Jul 5, 1951
Harris, Joel Chandler Dec 9 1845 – Jul 3, 1908
Harris, Sydney J. Sep 14, 1917 – Dec 8, 1986
Hawthorne, Nathaniel Jul 4, 1804 – May 19, 1864
Heller, Joseph May 1, 1923 – Dec 12, 1999
Hemingway, Ernest Jul 21, 1899 – Jul 2, 1961
Herbert, George Apr 3, 1593 – Mar 1, 1633
Holmes, Oliver Wendell Aug 29, 1809 – Oct 7, 1894
Hood, Thomas May 23, 1799 – May 3, 1845
Horace, Quintus Flaccus Dec 8, 65 BC – Nov 27, 8 BC
Hubbard, Elbert Jun 19, 1856 – May 7, 1915
Huxley, Aldous Jul 26, 1894 – Nov 22, 1963
Ionesco, Eugene Nov 26, 1909 – Mar 28, 1994
James, Henry Apr 15, 1843 – Feb 28 1916
Jefferson, Thomas Apr 2, 1743 – Jul 4, 1826
Johnson, Samuel Sept 18, 1709 – Dec 13, 1784
Jones, Ernest Jan 1, 1879 – Feb 11, 1958
Jones, Franklin 1908-1980
Jowett, Benjamin Apr 15, 1817 – Oct 1, 1893
Joyce, James Feb 2, 1882 – Jan 13, 1941
Kafka, Franz Jul 3, 1883 – Jun 3, 1924
Kavanagh, Patrick Oct 21, 1904 – Nov 30, 1967
Kazin, Alfred Jun 5, 1915 – Jun 5, 1998
Keats, John 1773 – Mar 5, 1852

Kelland, Clarence Budington 881 – Feb 18, 1964
Keller, Helen Jun 27, 1880 – Jun 1, 1968
Kennedy, John Fitzgerald May 29, 1917 – Nov 22, 1963
Knight, Eric Apr 10, 1897 – Jan 15, 1943
Koch, Kenneth Feb 27, 1925 – Jul 6, 2002
Kiernan, John Aug 2, 1892 – Dec 9, 1981
Kilpatrick, James Nov 1, 1920 – Aug 15, 2010
King, Jr, Martin Luther Jan 15, 1929 – Apr 4, 1968
Kingsley, Charles Jun 12, 1819 – Jan 23 1875
Kipling, Joseph Rudyard Dec 30, 1865 – Jan 18, 1936
Kunitz, Stanley Jul 29, 1905 – May 14, 2006
Lang, Andrew Mar 31, 1844 – Jul 20, 1912
Lao-tse 604 BC
Larkin, Philip Aug 9, 1922 – Dec 2 1985
Lawrence, D.H. Sep 11, 1885 – Mar 2, 1930
Lewis, Cecil Day Apr 27, 1904 – May 22, 1972
Lewis, C.S. Nov 29, 1898 – Nov 22, 1963
Lewis, Sinclair Feb 7, 1885 – Jan 10, 1951
Lindberg, Anne Morrow Jun 22, 1906 – Feb 7, 2001
Lofting, Hugh Jan 14, 1886 – Sept 26, 1947
Longfellow, Henry Wadsworth Feb 27, 1807 – Mar 24, 1882
Lowell, Amy Lawrence Feb 9, 1874 – May 12, 1925
Lynes, Russell Dec 2, 1910 – Dec 14, 1991
MacDonald, John Dann Jul 24, 1916 – Dec 28, 1986
MacLeish, Archibald May 7, 1892 – Apr 20, 1982
Mailer, Norman Jan 31, 1923 – Nov 10, 2007
Mann, Thomas Jun 6, 1875 – Aug 12, 1955
Marquis, Don Robert Jul 28, 1878 – Jun 16, 1937
Maugham, W Somerset Jan 25, 1874 – Dec 16, 1965
Maurier, Daphne May 13, 1907 – Apr 19, 1989
McLaughlin, Mignon Jun 6, 1913 – Dec 20, 1983
Melville, Herman Aug 1, 1819 – Sep 28, 1891
Mencken, Henry Louis Sep 12, 1880 – Jan 29, 1956
Michener, James A. Feb 3, 1907 – Oct 16, 1997
Miller, Henry Valentine Dec 26, 1891 – Jun 7, 1980
Milne, A. A. Jan 18, 1882 – Jan 31, 1956

Montgomery, Lucy Maude Nov 30, 1874 – Apr 24, 1942
Moore, George Augustus Feb 24, 1852 – Jan 21, 1933
Moore, Marianne Nov 15, 1887 – Feb 5, 1972
Morley, Christopher May 5 1890 – Mar 28, 1957
Nin, Angela Anais Juana Rosa Feb 21, 1903 – Jan 14, 1977
O'Connor, Flannery Mar 25, 1925 – Aug 3, 1964
O'Hara, John Jan 31, 1905 – Apr 11, 1970
Orwell, George Jun 25, 1903 – Jan 21, 1950
O'Shaughnessy, Arthur Wm Mar 14, 1844 - Jan 30, 1881
Ovid, Publius Mar 20, 43 BC – 17 AD
Pascal, Blaise Jun 19, 1623 – Aug 19, 1662
Parker, Dorothy Aug 22, 1893 – Jun 7, 1967
Peguy, Charles Jan 7, 1873 – Sept 4, 1914
Perkins, Maxwell Sep 20, 1884 – Jun17, 1947
Phelps, Austin Jan 7, 1820 – Oct 13, 1890
Plath, Sylvia Oct 27, 1932 – Feb 11, 1963
Plato 424 BC – 348 BC
Poe, Edgar Allan Jan 19, 1809 – Oct 7, 1849
Potter, Beatrix Jul 28, 1866 – Dec 22, 1943
Pound, Ezra Oct 30, 1885 – Nov 1, 1972
Pauling, Linus Feb 28, 1901 – Aug 19, 1994
Quintilanus, Marcus Fabius 35 – 100
Rand, Ayn Feb 20, 1905 – Mar 6, 1982
Rascoe, Arthur Burton Oct 22, 1892 – Mar 19, 1957
Renard, Pierre-Jules Feb 22, 1864 – May 22, 1910
Rilke, Rainer Maria Dec 4, 1875 – Dec 29, 1926
Roosevelt, Eleanor Oct 11, 1884 – Nov 2, 1962
Rosten, Leo Apr 11, 1908 – Feb 19, 1997
Rukeyser, Muriel Sep 15, 1913 – Feb 12, 1980
Rushkin, John Feb 8, 1819 – Jan 20, 1900
Sandburg, Carl Jan 6, 1878 – Jul 22, 1967
Saroyan, William Aug 31, 1908 – May 18, 1981
Seneca, Lucius Annaeus 4 – 65 AD
Sewell, Anna Mar 30, 1820 – Apr 25, 1878
Shaw, George Bernard Jul 26, 1856 – Nov 2, 1950
Shakespeare, William Apr 26, 1564 – Apr 23, 1616

Sheffield, John Duke of Buckingham Sep 8, 1647 – Feb 24, 1721
Shelley, Mary Aug 30, 1797 – Feb 1, 1851
Sibelius, Jean Dec 8 1965 – Sep 20 1957
Silverstein, Shel Sep 25, 1930 – May 9, 1999
Singer, Isaac Nov 21 1902 – Jul 24, 1991
Simenon, George Joseph Feb 13, 1903 – Sept 4, 1989
Smith, Dodie May 3 1896 – Nov 1990
Smith, Jack Aug 27, 1916 – Jan 9, 1996
Smith, Sidney Jun 3, 1771 – Feb 22, 1845
Smith, Walter Wellesley Sep 25, 1905 – Jan 15, 1982
Socrates 469 BC -399 BC
Sontag, Susan Jan 16, 1933 – Dec 28, 2004
Sophocles 497 BC – 405 BC
Southey, Robert Aug 12, 1774 – Mar 21, 1843
Speare, Elizabeth George Nov 21, 1908 – Nov 15, 1994
Spillane, Frank Mickey Mar 9, 1918 – Jul 17, 2006
Steele, Sir Richard Mar 12, 1672 – Sept 1, 1729
Stein, Gertrude Feb 3, 1874 – Jul 27, 1946
Steinbeck, John Feb 27, 1902 – Dec 20, 1968
Stegner, Wallace Feb 18, 1909 – Apr 13, 1993
Stevenson, Robert Louis Nov 13, 1850 – Dec 3, 1894
Stoker, Bram Nov 8, 1847 – Apr 20, 1912
Styron, William Jun 11, 1925 – Nov 1, 2006
Swift, Jonathan Nov 30, 1667 – Oct 19, 1745
Syrus, Publilius 43 BC
Tate, Allen Nov 19, 1899 – Feb 9, 1979
Teeters, Peggy Feb 8, 1918 – Jan 27, 2011
Thoreau, Henry David Jul 12, 1817 – May 6, 1862
Thurber, James Dec 8, 1894 – Nov 2, 1961
Tolkien, John Ronald Reuel Jan 3, 1892 – Sept 2, 1973
Tolstoy, Leo Sep 9, 1828 – Nov 20, 1910
Travers, Pamela Helen Aug 9, 1899 – Apr 23, 1996
Trollope, Anthony Apr 24, 1815 – Dec 6, 1882
Turgenev, Ivan Nov 9, 1818 – Sep 3, 1883
Twain, Mark Nov 30, 1835 – Apr 21, 1910
Updike, John Mar 18, 1932 – Jan 27, 2009

Virgil, Publilius Oct 15, 70 BC – Sep 21, 19 BC
Voltaire, Francois-Marie Nov 21, 1694 – May 30, 1778
Von Goethe, Johann Aug 28, 1749 – Mar 22, 1832
Vonnegut, Kurt Nov 11, 1922 – Apr 11, 2007
Vorse, Mary Heaton Oct 11, 1874 – Jun 14, 1966
Waugh, Arthur St. John Oct 28, 1903 – Apr 10, 1966
Walker, Margaret Jul 7, 1915 – Nov 30, 1998
Wells, H. G. Sep 21, 1866 – Aug 13, 1946
White, E.B. Jul 11, 1899 – Oct 1, 1985
Wiggin, Kate Douglas Sept 28, 1856 – Aug 24, 1923
Wilde, Oscar Oct 16, 1854 – Nov 30, 1900
Wilder, Laura Ingalls Feb 7, 1867 – Feb 10, 1957
Wilson, Ethel Jan 20, 1888 – Dec 22, 1980
Wilson, John 1785 – 1854
Woolf, Adeline Virginia Jan 25, 1882 – Mar 28, 1941
Wordsworth, William Apr 7, 1770 – Apr 23, 1850
Zola, Emile Apr 2, 1840 – Sep 29, 1902

www.ingramcontent.com/pod-product-compliance
Lightning Source LLC
Chambersburg PA
CBHW060232290526
45789CB00001B/21